WF

"Imagine sitting down with a wise and compassionate friend who guides you to a source of love and healing within you as near as your nightly dreams. "Those guys" may be smiling to know Mary Jo Heyen's deeply felt, clearly written book will open many hearts and minds to the potent wisdom of dreams. I will recommend it to many with enthusiasm."

— Marian Enochs Gay,
  Dream Practitioner

"I could have looked at this dream a thousand years and never seen it that way."

— dream workshop participant

"A simply written, understandable book about a complex subject. Mary Jo has explained the nature of Archetypal Dreamwork and its gifts in this book. If you have ever wanted to understand what your dreams are trying to tell you, this is a great place to start."

— C.K.,
  fellow dreamworker

"I've never been in this kind of conversation with another human being."

— dream workshop participant

WHO ARE

THOSE GUYS?

That Curious Sometimes Crazy
Cast of Characters Who Come to Us
Every Night in Our Dreams

MARY JO HEYEN

DAVEY PRESS

Davey Press
Printed in the United States of America
First Edition, 2015
Revised Edition, 2020

Cover Art: Greg Miles

CONTENTS

For my dad,
who knew the presence
of something greater than we are

It has only been a few years since the first edition of Who Are Those Guys? was published and much has been evolving in the way I work with dreams and dreamers.

Together, under the leadership of Rodger Kamenetz, along with inspired and dedicated dream colleagues, we have developed and established Natural Dreamwork. From our collective dreamwork of decades, thousands of dreams, offerings of dream presentations and workshops and most importantly the brave and tender hearts of dreamers, we continue to honor and follow our understanding of what it is our dreams want for us and of us. In our trust of the dreams and what they want to reveal to us our ways of being in relationship with them are a continual evolution.

Who Are Those Guys? was originally written as the companion piece to my dream workshop of the same name. Workshop participants, dream clients and other readers have expressed their desire to write notes along the way about their own dream characters. For example: What animals show up in my dreams? What are they doing? How do I feel in their presence? For this reason I have added "Dreams Images and Reflections" pages at the end of each chapter.

This is a short book, which didn't start out as a short book. It was meant to be a talk that could be included in the presentations and workshops that I offer on dreams. Along the way, it kept growing as all the curious cast of characters wanted to be included and I wanted them to have their presence here in these pages.

It is not meant to be a scholarly or comprehensive work on dreams, or even the dream characters themselves. It is not written with a voice of authority. It is meant to describe my experience and what I have learned from working with my own dreams and those of my clients. It speaks of how I step into dreams from an archetypal point of view and how I have developed both a relationship with and trust in this curious cast of dream characters.

My hope is that I have expressed this all in a way that will excite, inspire and invite readers into an exploration and conversation with their own dreams. Working with our dreams and ourselves it is a fluid work and we ... like our dreams themselves ... are ever changing ... ever revealing ... ever becoming.

THE
NATURAL DREAMWORK
APPROACH

While this is not a book about Natural Dreamwork
I do want to take some time here, in this second edition, to give you an overview of how it is we work
with dreams. The simplest way would be for me to
share with you as I do a new client, someone stepping
into their very first dream session.

YOUR DREAM WORLD

I would first invite you to tell me a bit about your
relationship with your dreams, how has this been
for you? Is your curiosity about your dreams something new or is it something that has been a long time
companion? You may want to take a moment here to
reflect on this unique and personal relationship.

CONFIDENTIALITY

What happens in a dream session is, of course, con-
fidential. I don't speak of it unless I have permission
and yet I encourage dreamers to share with whom-
ever they'd like…whatever they'd like. This brings
dream into their daily life conversations and helps
keep them alive and even inspires others to begin to
be in relationship with their own dreams.

TRUST

It takes time to build trust and yet our dreams don't wait. In a very first session a dream may reveal a deep hurt, loss or even violation. It can be startling for a new client to see and hear what is just underneath the surface of even a seemingly mundane dream. And I allow that time, assuring the dreamer that they don't have to answer a question immediately. As their trust in me and their dreams deepens, as the dreamer comes to know that their dreams want their healing this no longer is an issue and they become willing to share who they are, their wellness and their wounds.

DREAMWORK VERSUS TALK THERAPY

There is an interesting difference between traditional talk therapy and dreamwork. In talk therapy the client often brings in topics they would like to discuss, in a way setting the agenda. In dreamwork it is the dreams that set the agenda. The dream brings in topics we may indeed want to explore as well as topics we may not want to explore and yet the dreams invite us here...even in a very first session. And in doing this we aren't talking about a particular issue, which many of us can do quite well. We are exploring what is underneath a particular issue. We are immediately asked to be in a given moment...in a specific dream image, often a way we are in the world and to feel into it...to experience it. This is experiential work; it is visceral. It invites us into the opportunity to be fully embodied and fully en-souled. Even in a first session we can feel the power of this as we are in our body and in our hearts, aware of our feelings, perhaps feelings we haven't felt for a very long time.

ALIGNMENT

If I could only say one sentence to describe what it is our dreams want for us I would say, "Our dreams want to help us see where our inner and outer selves are or are not in alignment." How have we, by the mere fact of being born, regardless of our life experiences, lost connection to the truest part of who we are? Our dreams know how that happened and our dreams know how to help us come back into alignment.

RELATIONSHIP

If I could only say one word to describe what it is our dreams want for us I would say, "relationship." Dream by dream we are invited back into relationship with our true self, our soul, and from that deepest way of being we come into relationship with ourselves, each other and with the divine.

How do our dreams do all this?

DREAM CHARACTERS

Most of our dreams are filled with a cast of curious characters. They may be someone we know and reveal how it is we are in relationship to them. It may be someone we know or a stranger who is reflecting some part of us that the dream wants us to explore. And there may be those characters who are neither and may be, as theologian, Rudolph Otto refers to them in Chapter 9, the numinous, the Wholly Other.

SACRED ENCOUNTER

Dreams bring us into encounters with places, objects and beings. Some of these encounters are what we might call Sacred Encounters. In a dream moment we given the opportunity to feel something. Sometimes we do, we feel it deeply, and sometimes we miss the encounter. It's not that we've done something wrong but rather the feeling in that moment may feel too much. It could be fear or pain. It could be joy or love. The dreams know that something happened to us that taught us it wasn't okay to have these feelings and they invite us back into feeling. Our dreams come when we are ready to open to something. They do not ask too much of us but they do ask so much of us.

DREAM MEDICINE

There is a healing medicine found in every dream and that medicine is the recovery of our capacity to feel. We are invited in to the full palette of feeling…our love and pain, our joy and sorrow, our fear and vulnerability. For me, this capacity is one of the descriptions of soul. The soul feels it all. The actual potency of the soul is this capacity. What can a world do to someone who can feel everything?

SYMBOLS VERSUS IMAGES

Symbols are powerful and important. They immediately connect us to a meaning. They are kind of beautiful stand in for something bigger than they are. Images, especially those in our dreams, are approached differently than a symbol. We don't say that an image stands for something, but it does carry something. Images in our dreams carry feelings and these feelings want to be felt. An owl in our dream, for example, isn't explored as what the owl symbolizes in history and different cultures. We explore it as the encounter it is ... to be in the visceral presence of an owl and the feeling in that moment, a presence and an energy that is there for us.

CHALLENGING AND EGO PINCHING

Whether we had the best of life experiences or the worst there is something about taking birth that frays our connection to soul. Being human comes with a kind of forgetting the truth of who we are. We become conditioned. We learn what is accepted and valued and most of us try to conform to that. It is a safer way to live. We've learned to behave in ways that please others, caretake others and all at the expense of soul. We adapt to these expectations and in so doing forget the beauty of who it is we truly are.

A wound so many of us share is that we've learned to be cut off from our feelings...we so often truly don't know what we are feeling. We know how to react, have opinions and judgments about our lives, stories about our life...but we forgot how to feel our lives, this deeply meaningful embodied and ensouled way of living our lives. Our dreams want to help us remember. Dreams are an anamnesis, an unforgetting. In Natural Dreamwork we say that we bring dreams to life. I would like to extend that and say that our dreams bring us to life.

HORIZONTAL VERSUS VERTICAL

In working with dreams people often stay on the surface of the dream (the horizontal) exploring how the dream reflects what is going on in a person's life, even from the day before. Much of that may indeed be in the dream and yet in Natural Dreamwork we know the outer reflects the inner (and vice versa) and that dream is calling us to something underneath the surface, a deeper way of knowing ourselves and each other, a way that nourishes soul (the vertical.)

EXPLORATION

To explore a dream in its depth takes some time. I can't tell a dreamer what their dreams means because I don't know. What I can do is ask intentional curious questions, shine a light in dark corners, on a particular word, a space between words, all the while exploring, pausing, waiting until the dreamer might have that ahhh! moment of recognition. This is a moment of a return of memory and then of feeling … a recovery of feeling.

DREAM MOMENT

At the end of a dream session I will give the dreamer a practice to carry with them, a dream medicine or dream moment. It will reflect the deepest felt moment in our work that day. This is a kind of time-released medicine. As we spend some time in between sessions returning to the deeply felt moment we learn to stay open, be with and absorb the experience. It continues the inner conversation which is then responded to in subsequent dreams.

There is a scene from the film classic, "Butch Cassidy and the Sundance Kid," starring Paul Newman and Robert Redford. Butch and Sundance realize they are being relentlessly pursued by a posse. Every time they think they've eluded them, they look back and there they are. The posse will stop at nothing to bring them in.

SUNDANCE: *Who are those guys?*
BUTCH: *Aw...you're wasting your time (looking). They can't track us over rocks.*
SUNDANCE: *Tell them that.*
BUTCH: *"They're beginning to get on my nerves. Who are those guys?"*

Through the entire movie, Butch and Sundance are on the run, constantly looking back over their shoulders, only to see that whatever they do, wherever they go, they cannot outmaneuver or escape their pursuers. Instead they are always baffled, always questioning, "Who are those guys?"

So it is with us...relentlessly being chased night after night in our dreams by this curious cast of characters, causing us to be baffled like Butch and Sundance, to wake up, often times with a pounding heart or in a cold sweat. Who are those guys?

Who are those guys who can track us over rock, rout us out from our hiding places, against whom we can't lock the door, fly away to escape... those guys who just won't give up on reaching us?

Who is this curious cast of characters... guys who look like street people, like our beloved Uncle Charlie, or that annoying co-worker?

Who is this curious cast of dream characters who look, say and do outrageous things?

What if, instead of intending us harm as we often believe in our dreams, their relentless pursuit is really their strong desire to tell us something, to teach us something that really matters and most impor- tantly... *to feel something*... and in so doing, we begin to remember who it is we truly are. But since we're so busy running away from them, it takes a whole posse to get our attention, to bring us in.

And, like the movie posse, they don't give up. Each night we are met with this cast of characters, some we recognize, some we don't, some who charm us... some who scare the bejeezus out of us... a whole cast and crew intent on delivering the dream's message.

We ask ourselves... Who's orchestrating the dream? Who's working central casting? Choosing imagery? Who are those guys?

In these pages we will take a look at a unique way of stepping into our dreams, from an archetypal perspective, and from there offer insight into these dream figures, including our own dream ego and begin to sort out this curious cast of characters, who they might be and what it is they want for us.

Before we do that though, this feels like a good moment to speak about how to work with our dreams. Can we work with dreams on our own without the help and guidance of a dream practitioner? Well, yes, but a qualified yes. Part of the problem with working our dreams alone is that we don't know where we're stuck. We all have many blind spots where we can't quite see things clearly and it is invaluable to have the supportive and objective presence of someone familiar with the dream landscape and who can guide us through our dreams. What may look good in a dream may not be so good as you'll see in Chapter 4 on Dream Ego. To this day, I value the trusted presence of my own dream practitioner. There are moments, when working with one of my dreams, that the whole dream gets turned upside down and a wonderful teaching tumbles out, one I would not have seen on my own. I always want another pair of eyes and another heart looking at my dreams.

CHAPTER 1

DREAM BASICS

More unique than our fingerprints, more us than our DNA, are our dreams, because they change and grow as we change and grow. It's a nightly communication, individual and uniquely tailored for each of us.

So what are these dreams that we all have every night, often several of them, and why do they matter?

There is so much available research out there on dreams and the science of dreaming, it is not my intention to fill these pages with that research. I want to start with just one basic statistic...

Whether we remember them or not, we all do dream and we all have an average of four dreams per night, or about 1,460 dreams per year.

As written in Talmud... "An unexplored dream is like an unopened letter."

All of us are receiving close to 1,500 dream letters a year. Doing some simple math, take a person at age 65 and multiply that by 1,500 dreams. By age 65 we've received 94,900 of these nightly missives... and most of us never open them!

Joseph Campbell said that myth is the collective dream and the individual dream is the personal myth. All cultures have their own rich history of myths and many have captured our imagination. The world's myths are ways the cultures have tried to explain and teach what is universal, what is collective to all of us. There are even modern versions of these ancient myths that we mostly see in films, such as The Hunger Games, Star Wars, Batman, Whale Rider, Beasts of the Southern Wild and so many others.

Imagine your life as a movie, or better yet, an epic. It is. Each night your dreams are bringing your uniquely personal epic to you... really your myth. Dreams don't just want to bring the surface story of your life, important as that is. You already know that story. Your dreams want to bring to you what is *underneath* the story... the very reason your story is the unique story it is. Your dream is revealing the myth... your personal myth, the blueprint of your soul.

James Hillman said that myths are always being made and happening all around us, that we're always in our myth but that we don't know it. He said that even though we've lost connection to our personal myth we can't step out of it because it is our myth. If our dreams are bringing us our personal myth, then how can we discover and explore our personal myth? The answer seems clear ... through working with our dreams.

Each night a piece of our personal myth is revealed to us. The dreams are slowly separating out who it is we think we are versus who we truly are. Our inner teachers and lessons come disguised as this curious cast of characters ... and in working with our dreams they can begin to reveal themselves to us and what it is they want to teach us about ourselves.

Dream by dream, as we pay attention and absorb, we are shown what is not our true self. There's a wonderful word, apophatic, that I've used when teaching meditation. When we can drop into the silence, we begin learn who God is *by learning who God is not*. Our dreams can be seen as a form of the apophatic as they often teach us who we are *by teaching us who we are not*. The dream slowly peels back the layers of persona and our misunderstandings to reveal our true self, the self we lost connection to and even forgot we were. It's an invitation to clear our mind and open our hearts, offering us the choice to engage with ourselves and to be in relationship with this deeper part of who we truly are, to be in relationship with the divine and *from that core place* to be in relationship with others and our world.

Dreams can be loving, terrifying, and laugh out loud funny ... and they are always self revealing. They all come with the intention to heal those parts of ourselves that have been wounded and to remind us that we all have inner love and support.

The dream reveals both the state of our outer life and the state of our inner life ... and shows where the inner and outer are out of alignment. The dreams want to re-connect us with something that we have lost and while I believe that 'something' is our soul, the reason we work with our dreams varies for each person. For some, it may mean a desire for more wholeness, to simply be more aware and happier in life, to have better relationships. For some, dream-work can be a type of therapy that can help unravel and break unwanted lifelong patterns. Dreams are the guide for helping heal those parts of ourselves that we know are broken, and perhaps, more importantly, those parts that we don't know are broken. We've been gone from our true inner home for so long we've forgotten who we are and how we can be. For others, it can be a support for a current spiritual practice, or a spiritual practice in itself, deepening the connection with our true self and the inner support of the divine.

So many of us feel that niggle, that something is just not quite right but we don't know how to name it and heal it on our own ... the dreams do. Those who have developed a trust in their dreams, trust their importance and their intention and willingly step towards these nightly messages from the dreamworld.

My own work with dreams is through the lens of the archetypal as it, more than any other way I've experienced dreams, unravels for me the mystery that is my dreams. It helps me begin to understand and remember these curious sometimes crazy characters and answer the question, "Who are those guys?" and what it is they are trying to teach me.

CHAPTER 2

MY JOURNEY INTO DREAMS

DREAM *(age 4)*
"I am standing at the top of our stairs in my childhood home. I feel a movement in my upper stomach (solar plexus), lift up and float down the stairs to the bottom landing. What fun! I climb back up and do it again ... and again."

Since age four, with that first remembered dream, I have had a steady and close relationship with my dreams, a lifelong curiosity. I knew they were trying to tell me something, but I just didn't know what ... and couldn't seem to find out.

As I look back, even in this first seemingly fun dream as a four year old, there was something the dream was showing me. It wasn't until over sixty years later that I realized the gift in this dream. I was invited to speak about dreams and grief with a grief support group, all of whom had lost a loved one within the past year. In our first meeting, I explained what support and insight we can find in our dreams. For the second meeting we were going to work with some of their recent dreams. On my way to this second meeting it hit me full on. In my very first dream, at age four, there was unfelt grief. I remember getting up that morning over sixty years ago, and trying to repeat my flight down the stairs. I couldn't understand why I couldn't feel the bubble of energy in my the middle of my stomach that would allow me to lift off. I was confused and sad. In that moment, as an inarticulate child, I sensed there was some way I had known myself that was no longer available to me. I was now separated from it and didn't know how to get it back…I felt grief. Already, at the tender age of four, my dreams were teaching me, wanting me to remember my connection to my soul.

Over the next six decades, I recorded my dreams, in journals, on scraps of paper, studying all dream-related material as best I could given a busy career has an educator.

Finally, when I retired from teaching, I began a concentrated study of dreams. As I mentioned in the Introduction, there are many wonderful theories, teachers and schools exploring the meaning of our dreams...yet nothing was quite calling me into the dream the way I desired.

Allow me a bit of a segue here. In my twenties, already with a daily meditation practice, I had a 'knowing' during one early 4:00 a.m. sitting that I would have to wait until my sixties for my heart's desire. A hard thing for a twenty-something to hear but I trusted it. So, I continued my inner work, studying different paths, including being a longtime student of Buddhism and meditation...and I waited, trusting that early morning 'knowing.'

I didn't realize it at the time, having turned sixty, but not only was I nearing the end of my waiting for my heart's desire, that desire would be found through my lifelong elusive companions...my dreams.

A pattern of sleep for me has always been to wake up around midnight, get up and sit for a while in the quiet. After I retired I no longer had my alarm set for 4:00 a.m., so my late nights, sitting in our loft, began to include journaling, reading and listening to podcasts on dreams. This is such a treasured time for me that I even call it 'my midnight loft.'

One cold January night, I woke up as usual, went to the loft and found I was near the end of my podcast list...so I tuned in to one I had put off for almost a year. It was called "Archetypal Dreamwork" and I had postponed listening to it because I assumed it was more about the work of Carl Jung, from which I had already learned so much. Yet, I was still hopeful for something to call me more personally into my dreams so I took a listen.

This podcast on an archetypal approach to dreams was an interview with a fellow named Rodger Kamenetz. I did not know who Rodger was, that he had written the bestselling book, "The Jew in the Lotus," his account of accompanying a delegation of rabbis to Dharamsala, India to meet with the Dalai Lama. His Holiness wanted to learn from the rabbis how a people survive in exile. I also did not know that he had written a book about his own journey with dreams, "The History of Last Night's Dream" as featured on Oprah's Soul Series. I knew nothing other than the voice I was hearing on that podcast in my dark midnight loft, what he was saying about what our dreams want for us, how they come to heal, to support us and to reconnect us to those parts of ourselves to which we had lost connection. I listened to him speak about the characters in the dreams and how they guide him as he works with the dreams of his own dream clients.

Here was the language, the heart...*the soul*...of the dream I had been searching for and desired to learn. Two days later I became one of Rodger's dream clients.

I also went into an intense training program with, what was at the time, The Center for Archetypal Dreamwork, based on the work of Marc Bregman, founder of a unique way of working with dreams.

Now, as a Natural Dreamwork Practitioner, with my own practice, I continue to work with dreams from this archetypal perspective.

And what is that archetypal perspective? In working with dreams in this way, it is seen that every dream has an intention and a desire to re-connect us to that from which we have been separated … and that is the separation from our soul.

Along the way, sometimes through trauma, sometimes just in living, we lose touch with the truest part of who we are. We have forgotten who we truly are and begin to believe we are the persona we have developed in order to feel safe and part of the world at large.

Still so many of us have that nagging sense that we don't belong, that something ineffable is missing in our lives. Something *is* missing. We have lost the connection to our soul and we have lost our connection to the divine. Working with the material that comes to us in our dreams, especially in this archetypal approach, we begin to learn where there are tears in the fabric of our being and we can begin to repair them.

Many dream schools, helpful as they are, stay on the surface of the dream, what we call the horizontal, and try to understand the dream only from the way it relates to the outer world. For example, test anxiety in a dream means there's anxiety in your current life and dreams can help you take a look at that anxiety.

All very true, but stepping in with an archetypal perspective, the dream doesn't stop there. It works with that and then very quickly turns from the horizontal to the vertical...true depth work...using the outer situations, issues and dilemmas to teach us about the *inner situation*, of how we lost connection to our soul and to the divine. So test anxiety on the surface begins to reveal the deeper anxiety of lost connection to our inner support which is reflected in our anxious feeling that we are alone in this world without support.

For me, a core quality of the soul is to 'love and to be loved,' and if that's true, then how did we all get so far from this? And a question that is even more important...how do we get back? Again, every dream has an intention and if there is one intention the dream has, if there is a road back, it is to feel our lost and unfelt feelings.

CHAPTER 3

FEELINGS

A whole chapter dedicated to feelings? If I were to add a second question to the theme of this book, "Who are Those Guys?" it would be "What is it those guys want?"…and the answer is…Feel Your Feelings.

When I speak about lost connection to our soul…to the divine…what is the nature of that connection? It is about the soul's capacity to feel…to feel it all. The soul, unlike us, doesn't pick and choose what it will feel. The soul *feels it all*, love, pain, fear, joy, loss, sadness, tenderness and sensuality…all of it. If we cut ourselves off and won't feel our pain then we've cut ourselves off from feeling the love as well. Why? Because the depth of our ability to feel love is reflected in the depth of our ability to feel pain.

As we open our hearts to feel more, we become a

vessel that can contain it all. As we gain trust in our dreams, in what the archetypes want for us, we learn to stay with difficult feelings as they arise. Our usual approach to this is to believe that *we* need to move through our feelings, often giving ourselves a time-line to feel and then move on from them. Can you feel the harshness in that, the ego and the persona? Instead, when we learn to trust what is arising, we also learn to trust that our feelings will neither over-whelm us nor take us out. We learn that feelings, even very difficult ones, such as grief and great loss, not only need and want to move through us, they know *how* to move through us in their own way... and in their own wisdom... *how to be felt all the way through.* We feel them in our heart... and in our body. It's a vis-ceral experience. We can arrive at a place where we actually welcome the arising feeling, difficult as it may be, because we know we are opening the long-closed channels that connect us to the divine and to the inner support that waits for us there.

This piece alone, to feel our feelings, is the core to the heart of working with our dreams. I've been fortunate to receive a number of powerful teach-ings on the importance of our feelings and they have impacted my life tremendously from how I meditate to how I am in relationship with myself, others and the divine.

One teaching was through the extensive train-ing to become a dream practitioner. We stepped into hundreds of dreams and learned how to tell the difference between what we would call a feeling versus an emotion, which I will refer to as essential and non-essential feelings.

Even before this I learned a truly sacred teaching, which came from an old out of print book I found lying in an ignored box at a used book sale. It was about the work of a 13th century mystic, Jan van Ruysbroeck. There was a kernel of his work that taught me so much about respecting and being with feelings as they arise. For him, a quality of what it means to be a true mystic is that we have the capacity to feel our feelings and then to know that it is through our feelings the divine communicates with us, that our feelings are the conversation with the divine.

Our dreams bring us all our feelings, either as they are expressed clearly in the dream or where they lie hidden in some gap in the dream, as yet unfelt.

We learn to discriminate between what is an *essential* feeling (part of our eternal essence), such as love and pain and what is a *non-essential* feeling such as righteousness, reactive anger and jealousy. These reactions (a feeling with a story attached) don't have true substance and once thoroughly explored begin to dissolve. At first they are mostly the only way we know ourselves and we are willing to feel these non-essential feelings, even if they don't make us happy, because we mistakenly think they are feelings, and well, that's how life is. However, in believing this we let them distract and keep us from feeling our essential feelings, which we are afraid to feel. This is our capacity to feel love, to receive love, to feel our pain and our true joy. We are afraid they will be too much, we are afraid we will be too much. It feels safer to stay with the non-essential feelings that are lying on top of what is essential in us. The dreams can help us learn to discriminate between the two and then we can begin to recover what is underneath, our essential selves.

I had an amazing first experience with this years ago and didn't know at the time how important it was. Into day two of a meditation retreat, long hours of sitting, I received a beautiful inner teaching. I suddenly saw in my mind's eye a beautiful, low, black lacquered table sitting in front of my meditation cushion. An inner guidance showed me what to do, so on the table I 'laid' a strong negative opinion I had about someone and asked myself, "Am I still me without this opinion?" Of course, the answer was yes, so in a mental sweeping of my arm, I swept the opinion off the table. Huh...still me. So began a lengthy laying on the table of judgements, opinions, ideas I had about others, about myself, who I thought I was and needed to be. None were standing up to the question, "Am I still me without this…?" The time between the question and the answer slowly lengthened, became more difficult, closer to the bone. Then came the questions, "Am I still me without kindness?"…"without the ability to feel sadness or pain?" "Am I still me without love?" Each time the answer was 'No.' I would not be me without these essential feelings. Not only would I not be me, I wouldn't want to exist without those qualities. I realized later that I had arrived at those feelings of my essential self.

What would later become core to my work with dreams was previewed for me in that meditation. Essential feelings are part of who we are in our essence, our soul and to which the dream wants to return us. That would seem to mean that when I refuse to feel my fear, my vulnerability, my pain, my loss ... I'm not my real me ... and I want to be real me.

The Someone or Something that I consider the divine feels love, feels sadness, feels joy, feels pain. As I recover my ability to feel it all, all the essential feelings, I recover my ability to be not only in deeper connection with my soul and this divinity, I am learning that to be able to feel all my feelings is to be, as mystic Van Ruysbroeck experienced, in conversation with my soul and with the divine. *Essential feelings are the conversation between me, my soul and the divine.*

CHAPTER 4

THE DREAM EGO

DREAM

*"I am skating along an upper balcony of a
building, trying to avoid small frozen pools,
worried that I will break through the ice.
Below, I see a large elk lying on the ground being
attacked by another elk. His side has a huge gash,
opened and bloody. There is a large crowd of
people watching. A young man is walking back
to a waiting car carrying the elk's bloody rack of
antlers. I am horrified. From the balcony, I yell,
"That's against the law!" It turns into a chant
that the others pick up ... in unison we all chant,
"That's against the law!"*

I imagine if this dream were to have gone on any longer I would have had the crowd making posters and picketing the place in protest. This was one of the very first dreams worked when I began archetypal dreamwork. I couldn't wait to explore its meaning in session with Rodger. I was sure that he would compliment me, say what a great steward I am of the National Park System! Well, it didn't quite go that way, didn't quite go that way at all. I'll come back to this dream in a moment.

Our own presence in our dreams is what we can call the 'dream ego.' We are in the dream as ourselves, usually our current age, our current state of mind, behaving as we behave in the outer world.

The dream ego reveals all the ways we are in the world. It shows us ways we are that support and are in alignment with our soul, where we feel love and can feel loved … feel connected to something bigger than we are. However, when we begin working with our dreams what we're mostly shown are ways we are in the world that actually block this inner connection.

One way the dream ego does this is by showing us how our mind works … and very quickly I might add … to make sense of a situation, to find an explanation, to create and believe a story so that we can be okay with ourselves in the world … and that story is what helps us avoid seeing and feeling into something difficult … what it is the dream wants for us.

This is what makes working with our dreams so

challenging. It is very 'ego pinching' to see ourselves as controlling, petty, mean or selfish. The dream doesn't worry about stepping on our toes. It shows us exactly as we are, it exposes the ways we react, judge, hide…how we avoid feeling what it is in us that wants to be felt. It shows not only where we've been broken but helps us understand how we were broken.

The dream also shows us ways we are that we thought were good for us, that the world may love about us, but that don't serve our soul. It shows us these blind spots…those parts of ourselves that we thought were us versus who we truly are.

For example, for many people, both men and women, a blind spot that shows up right away in dreams is how we caretake others. On the surface it can seem wonderful that we put the needs of others in front of our own; how unselfish of us. But as we approach these dreams from the archetypal perspective, the dream goes from horizontal to vertical and we find that we begin to feel the oppressive weight of responsibility for the happiness of others. We may even have an underlying resentment that we don't want to feel. In this kind of caretaking we are often doing for others not only what they can do for themselves but what they *can and should* be doing for themselves and their own soul. We are actually hindering them from the opportunity to find their own way through to connection with their soul. And the outer world can have a big reaction to us if we take a moment and ask ourselves what is it that our own soul needs in order to flourish and be expressed in the world and then begin that exploration for ourselves. Often, the recipients of our caretaking don't like it when we start to learn from our dreams that this caretaking behavior is neither meeting the needs of our soul nor the needs of the ones being caretaken. My experience has been that for most they come to accept this and even embrace. They begin to explore their own needs and desires and give themselves permission to express them in the world.

There is another really important piece we need be aware of as we begin to work with our dreams. How many of us, in our desire for wholeness and happiness, throw our hands up to the divine and say, "Just tell me what to do and I'll do it!" Much to our chagrin, the divine doesn't seem to work that way...and neither do our dreams. Why doesn't the dream just tell us what to do in clear and simple language? A mystery and a marvel of our dreams is that they will *show* us how we are but they won't tell us *what to do*. Once shown, it is then our choice, to learn from the message of the dream and begin to work with it, feeling into it, changing and growing from the inside out. It is always our choice.

Which brings us back to the dream that opened this chapter. This dream which I titled, 'The Bloody Elk,' is full of characters, each bringing a teaching about how I have been in the world.

My dream ego is skirting around frozen ice pools, afraid to break through to the water below... and what is in the water below? Feelings I don't want to feel. How do I keep myself from feeling them? Well, there are many ways we can do that but for me I found causes, good versus bad, right versus wrong, fair versus unfair. This can all look very good in the outer world. Things get done, causes get served... all the while my connection to my soul was lying under small easily avoided pools of ice. I had learned how to react to what I felt was unjust, to tell myself that I was speaking and acting for those who couldn't speak and act for themselves, that this was righteous indignation. The truth was that this was a false feeling, a non-essential feeling keeping me from the unfelt essential feeling that was underneath.

The glowing gift of the dream, which I couldn't yet see, was for me to see the wounded and bloodied elk... and to feel it as my own wounded self. When Rodger, my dreamwork practitioner, asked me what I felt about the elk, all I could say was that I felt badly, but nothing much deeper. I never thought the hardest question I would be asked in my life was, "What are you feeling?" I had nothing. I had learned to have thoughts, ideas, opinions and judgments ("That's against the law!") all of which could look and sound like true feelings... but weren't.

My feelings, my essential feelings, were lying under pools of frozen ice.

And yet our dreams are very kind, challenging but kind. The dreams knew that it was too soon to show me as the one with a painful gaping wound, so it created a character: the image of an elk lying on the ground with a bloody wound. The dream also showed my persona self raising its fist in outrage at an injustice. This was the way I could be in the world; it was a blind spot.

Our dreams aren't saying don't defend the weak. They aren't saying don't speak up for those who can't speak for themselves. What they are saying is to feel into our own wound, our own pain, our own loss ... *and from that place* ... speak for what is true and needs healing in ourselves and the world.

As we listen and learn from what it is our dreams want for us something remarkable happens. We find that we change both in our dreams and in our outer world. We heal from the inside out. We begin to have dreams where we are less reactive with a need to control. We become more willing to be vulnerable without the need to know and manage everything. These inside changes in our dreams are reflecting ways we're changing in our outer world, and we not only heal into ourselves, we heal in our relationships and can be with ourselves and others in a truer and more honest way.

As we come into alignment with the soul, qualities we thought we'd lost for good ... true joy, sensuality, creativity, our ability to feel the full range of emotions from deepest pain to deepest love … all begin to return to us as we recover our true self … our soul self.

CHAPTER 5

SOME OF THOSE GUYS

It's not often that we are alone throughout an entire dream. That in itself is a very tender and meaningful dream to explore. Most times there are at least one or two... or a whole crew of other characters who show up to help us, annoy us... *and always*... to teach us.

Some of them are familiar people... our spouses, our children, friends, co-workers, even famous people. Some of them are unfamiliar. A client may describe a dream character as 'a woman, 50's, friendly, good feeling about her' or 'a man, bearded, 60's, stern.' Some of these characters may be our inner teachers, which I'll discuss in Chapter 9, The Archetypes.

Some of these characters may really be coming into the dream as themselves. Perhaps we have a dream with our partner and we are involved in some activity. In working the dream we would find out how this is for you. Is the dream portraying this aspect of your relationship as something satisfying and fulfilling... or is it showing you some place where there is an unresolved conflict, a lack of desire or connection? The dream may want to show you that you not only lost connection to some vital part of yourself, but that you've forgotten it was ever yours.

Some figures in a dream can seem very negative and we don't want to be around them, they make us feel icky... or they feed our ego in a way that makes us feel good but isn't good for our soul. Often they come into our dreams as mirrors that are reflecting ways we are in the world, but either have a blind spot about or are in denial.

I worked briefly with a woman client who had dreams where a snippy, terse woman kept showing up. When I asked her gently if there is any way that she is also that way, she said, snippily and tersely, "Everyone says I'm wonderful." To consider that any part of herself was less than wonderful was too much for her ego to bear... too painful to let in.

Many of us have experienced shame, abandonment, abuse and loss as children. In order to survive, our child selves created an ego that could cope with the outer world pain and through necessity we developed a persona that could protect and armor us from anyone or anything that might threaten. However, we pay a high price for that persona... too high a price.

We come to believe that the persona we unknowingly built is our true self. It's not, it's really a thick barrier not only between us and the world, but between us and our soul.

Our dreams, if we let them, will begin to break through this barrier and challenge us. They tell us the truth of who we are. They already know everything about us, where we're whole, where we're broken, where we're stuck. We may not want to admit any of this to ourselves, believing the world only sees what we want them to see. We're only fooling ourselves. Not only our dreams, but other people already know many of these things about us, things we won't admit or don't want to know about ourselves.

Yet... if we begin to trust our dreams and can take the pinch to the ego, and be willing to squirm a bit, we can begin to see and feel into these painful behaviors we have acquired and begin to heal them. We can't heal what we won't reveal. No one wants to be mean or caustic... it is a covering that we have developed over the years as a way to protect the tender wound that is underneath the abrasive behavior. The dreams want to help us separate from this false sense of self. The first step, however, is we have to be willing to look at what the dreams are offering and recognize how we behave in these painful ways — ouch!

The same is true for beautiful soul-filled qualities. Many of us have lost our connection to our true desire, our libido (our sexuality, sensuality, creativity) and have mistaken our acquired personas for our true selves. We believe it is normal to feel alienated, alone and empty sometimes to the point of numbness or even nihilism. *We believe it is normal to not feel.* Our dreams want to show us how we aren't living from our true selves, and they do that by bringing into our dreams characters that mirror that forgotten quality.

So the dream characters may come as children, as outrageous characters that are having a ball at doing what we no longer allow ourselves: running, singing, dancing, challenging the status quo, breaking rules, saying 'no' to a dark energy, saying 'yes' to a rising joy. These beautiful feelings and ways of being aren't meant just for the dreamworld. They are reminders of what we have lost, of who we are and who we can still be in our life.

We may see someone in a dream with qualities that we admire and that inspire us … maybe even frighten us. We wake up thinking, 'I could never be like that.' The dream character wants to help us remember this part of ourselves. We've been separated for so long we have forgotten that these gorgeous qualities are ours as well. To recover them feels frightening and so we project them onto others. Jungian, Robert Johnson, says that we ask others to hold the beauty of who we are … *our gold* … until we can hold it for ourselves. The dreams want us to remember and take back our gold.

CHAPTER 6

OUR DEAD

There is a very special category of dreams that imme-diately has meaning for the dreamer, and that is when we have dreams of our dead, whether it is a parent, a grandparent, a partner, a child. We want and welcome those dreams that have someone we love who is no longer with us physically. I work with grief support groups and almost without exception the bereaved not only want, they wait hopefully for a dream of their deceased loved one.

Why do they come to us in our dreams? Is it unfin-ished business? While it may not always be the case, we often find that the deceased person in the dream really seems to embody the presence of our loved one and they seem to be coming with a very specific inten-tion for the dreamer.

They often come in ways to show us that they are indeed fine and this can be an important thing for us to know especially if they died at a young age, through a sudden death or through illness. They want to bring some kind of comfort, support and assurance, so they often come in ways that radiate health and can be a comfort that, not only does life continue on into the after life, but also that the loving connection endures.

The deceased may also come into our dreams for similar reasons as the archetypes do...to teach us something...to encourage us. They certainly already have a leg up on the situation as we don't tend to run away from them. We recognize them, we trust them... and we love them. We are more ready to receive their message.

If the dream has someone with whom we had a difficult relationship we can find these dreams especially upsetting and frightening and would require the careful exploration that any dream of this kind would need.

Since the first edition of this book so much has evolved around my own work the dreams of the dead. I am a hospice volunteer, part of the hospice team, their dream specialist, working with patients and their families. Even for those who previously didn't pay much attention to their dreams, an impending death, whether one's own or that of a loved one, can create a new urgency and poignancy with regards to dreams. End of life dreams can offer a healing presence, an ability to be with our fear and not be overcome by it, a release from what has weighed on us, offering support and even a helping hand across the mysterious threshold.

CHAPTER 7

ANIMALS

Just as humans who show up in our dreams, animals also carry certain qualities that want to evoke some feeling and awakening in us. A weakness in a dream dictionary is that it will often assign only one or two qualities to an animal. We can be left feeling that the image and feeling it evoked in our dream doesn't fit. Just as different dream characters have individual meanings for the dreamer, different animals mean different things to different people. There really isn't a 'one size fits all.' So it is true with animals. A cat for one person may be a loving and comforting friend in waking reality and in the dream. For others a cat may represent indifference and aloofness.

Each animal, as it appears in a given dream, needs to be explored from the dreamer's own experience.

However, there does seem to be a common thread running through what particular animals *may* be representing. Our response (read: reaction) to it in our dream reveals yet another piece about our relationship with our inner self. I'll mention a few animals here with the reminder that the experience of them and the gifts they bring into the dreams is through an archetypal dreamwork lens.

Some creatures in our dreams are very aligned with the archetypal world, reflecting parts of ourselves we have forgotten or lost.

Do we still know that part of ourselves that can be with something more powerful than we are, can stand in the presence, intensity and confidence of a mountain lion, feel our fear and awe and not run away?

When a mother bear and her cubs show up in our dreams, can we feel her fierce love for her cubs, and know that it is reflecting the fierce love that is felt for us and our soul? Or do we run away from her and this part of ourselves, not believing that we can be loved in this way?

Think of the power and energy that a horse represents...our libido (creativity, passion, sensuality.) When horses are in our dreams do we ride with this powerful energy or does it frighten us?

Dogs seem to be very connected to the archetypal world. Often in our dreams they want us to follow them. They seem to know the direction we need to head. Yet, in our dreams we may have our dogs on leash. We try to control what should not be controlled by us. As we develop inner trust we learn to trust a dog's wisdom and follow where they want to lead us…back to the archetypal, to our inner teachers and the relationship we can have with them.

Snakes in the section on archetypal animals? More than any other creature, snakes seem to evoke a strong visceral response, from repulsion to fear. They really have gotten a bad rap. Snakes are primordial energy, an ancient presence that comes up from the unconscious, with material that can be frightening for us to look at, so we often turn away. Snakes don't close their eyes to what is arising. They want to communicate this wisdom to us through their bite, again fear-invoking as we don't understand their intention. Their bite, which is painful, wants to kill in us what is not of our soul…it is poison only to our ego.

Understandably, when we come upon a lion, a tiger, bear or a snake and other animals in a dream it can be frightening. So we often head in the opposite direction, want to tame them…or worse, kill them. We don't understand what it is they are trying to teach us.

For example, if a dreamer has a frightening dream where they are being chased by a tiger and are convinced they are going to be eaten by the tiger, during session, as the practitioner I would ask the dreamer, "Can you stop running, turn to the tiger, feel your fear and stand in that moment?" Then we would explore what comes up in that moment. The dreamer may still feel fear but there may be new feelings arising, such as excitement, potency and energy. These wild animals reflect the potent, awe inspiring energy of the archetypal realm. This is raw, untamable energy; it can and should be a frightening experience. However, they are also part of the invitation back to our soul and our connection to the divine. We are in the presence of something greater than ourselves.

Other animals may display qualities that reflect places we are still stuck and separated from our soul. Some can make us laugh about ourselves, others are more treacherous on our soul journey. Again, with most images in our dreams we want to understand what the particular images means to the dreamer and honor that relationship.

It's not happenstance that the image of monkeys is used for beginning meditators who find difficulty in quieting their mind. It's even called, "monkey mind." Imagine the sight and feeling of monkeys jumping through tree branches. Yes, we can recognize this scattered energy in ourselves and begin to work with it.

Spiders hold a sacred place in many traditions including the Navajo and we want to be aware of those associations when working a dream. Spiders themselves, like snakes are misunderstood and feared. For many of us though spiders can be an image of how we are spun in a web of who we think we are which keeps us separate not only from our true self but our ability to be in true relationship with others. We get caught up in the spider's tale, which keeps us lost in story, all the while draining us of our creativity and libido.

Think of how reptiles, such as crocodiles and alligators exist...just under the surface of the water, lurking...ready to snap their jaws. Is there a way we're like that with ourselves and others? Do we lie in wait ready to suddenly leap...to anger, to judgments and reaction?

There are so many more animals that show up in our dreams and they each carry so much potential for knowing ourselves better. Again, each dreamer can, through working with their dream, discover what the personal answer may be for them. Is the rabbit in your dream reflecting your shyness and gentleness or is it showing you how you have lost your voice and can't speak?

Next time you have an animal in your dream know that they, like the human characters, come to teach you something about yourself.

CHAPTER 8

CHILDREN

In an archetypal approach to dreamwork we have learned to pay particular attention to children in our dreams, because we've learned that they often carry and reflect an aspect of our soul. How we see them and relate to them in our dreams is often a reflection of how we are in relationship to our soul.

Are the children in our dreams innocent and vulnerable? Do they have a joie de vivre? Are they supported and loved by other characters in the dream? Are they children being children?

Or are the children in our dreams afraid, lost and hurt? Is there a sense of neglect, abandonment and loss? Are they somehow damaged? Do we dislike them?

All of us, whether we were raised in the most

loving of homes or suffered the worst kind of trauma imaginable, have experiences in life that cause a separation between us and our connection to our soul. Dreams will allude to experiences and memories that came with us into this life. We all have parts of us that are broken, some worse than others, and the dreams know what these are and how to heal them.

We can look at our life and ask ourselves...are we able to be in our tenderness and vulnerability, the child to something bigger than ourselves, and let that be present in the world? Or do we hide and protect that part of ourselves because it has been hurt and we fear we will be hurt again, and so live from a place of mistrust and separation?

While the soul is complete and whole in and of itself, it often shows up in our dreams in two forms of expression...a boy child and a girl child. They are often young children, age 7 and under...the place of innocence and connection to the divine...the eternal age of the soul. They also come as teens full of the exuberance and openness that is teen energy.

The soul qualities that the boy energy carries are strong presence, a sort of 'am-ness.' He is all boy, doesn't ask for permission and knows what he wants, and knows who he is. He carries our creativity, our libido. Libido doesn't just mean sexual drive or energy. Yes, it is our sexuality, but it is also our passion and sensuality. It is our creativity and desire to express ourselves and to experience others and the world. The boy has a strong voice that speaks clearly. He is all this because he knows he is loved and is in relationship with the divine. When these qualities are wounded and we can't let them be in the world, we say that 'the boy has lost his voice.' We have come to believe that it isn't safe to express these boy qualities and so we adapt and we adopt other, more accepted qualities and so our persona is shaped...and sadly this false self is who we believe we are.

The soul qualities of the girl are all about relation-ship...our desire to love and to be loved. The girl car-ries our ability to be vulnerable, to feel it all, to speak the truth...from our heart. The girl, too, knows she is loved by the divine. Her voice is the voice of the soul and she is the soul in its potency. And like the boy, when that part of us is wounded, she no longer speaks...it isn't safe. So again, in order to survive in the world, we are conditioned by our wounds to develop aggressiveness, toughness, rightness...all the while the girl soul remains underneath...and we are unable to be in true relationship without her.

When we don't have the true heart-connected support of a father or a mother who loves us, or worse shames and diminishes us, we come to believe we are alone in the world. We have lost the connection and the ability to be in our soul, children of the divine, loved and supported. Instead, we become good man-agers, of ourselves, others and our feelings. We have lost our ability to trust. We become the 'adults in charge,' not asking for help, even believing there is no help to be had.

Again, that is why we may often see damaged children in our dreams, children that are angry, ill, abandoned and sometimes even dead. These children mirror what happened to our connection with our soul. Often we are afraid of them, don't want to be around them, perhaps we're even angry at them. It is safer to be angry at this part of ourselves than to recover it. We are angry at them because we are afraid of what it is they ask of us. We believe if we are willing to be vulnerable, to speak our truth we will once again be hurt or abandoned, or even worse, annihilated. It takes time to repair, and our dreams know this. They carefully keep bringing us dreams that help us recover ourselves.

However it is, and to whatever degree it is, we all came to be wounded and hurt. We then learned to live from that defended place in the world and it is important to remember that the soul ... through all the hardships and trauma we may have experienced ... remains untouched, intact. The soul is still in its fullness, innocence and relationship with the divine. We are just separated from it. Our dreams help us bridge and heal this gap and return to this truth of who we are.

When we do begin to heal, we discover that true potency lies in our ability to be vulnerable ... our ability to feel our hurt, our love and our pain. We know that to be in the human experience means we will indeed be hurt again, feel deep pain ... but our dreams help us recover the knowing ... the true embodied, ensouled knowing that we are not alone.

Imagine a divine figure you hold in highest esteem from your own religious or spiritual perspective. Is there any essential feeling that being won't feel? Isn't the very reason that they can feel love, pain, joy, sorrow, the reason we trust them, the reason we know they understand us, because they themselves have experienced what it is we are feeling? We, too, can return to the wholeness of who we are, the eternal children of the divine and know that we are loved and supported unconditionally. This is what inner support feels like ... we love and we know we are loved.

CHAPTER 9

THE ARCHETYPES

This is the bottom line answer to the question, "Who are those guys?'

There are many ways that the word archetype is used in philosophy, psychology and anthropology. They may refer to archetypes as a constantly recurring symbol or motif in literature, painting, or mythology. It may be a pattern of behavior, thought or image, the fundamental characteristics of something. Jung referred to archetypes as the collectively inherited unconscious idea that is universally present in individual psyches. See... it starts to get heady, doesn't it? Again, so much is available in research and literature that I would do a disservice by trying to explain archetypes here other than how we use the term in Natural Dreamwork and how I have come to experience them *personally* in my dreams and my clients' dreams.

Of all the characters that come in our dreams, it is the archetypes who are most likely not a part of us. These are often those whose presence is so strong that they may even wake us up from the dream with a feeling so intense that it can stay with us for hours, days and even years later. They may come as beings of light or they may come as outrageous characters, doing and saying provocative and challenging things... often the very ones we are quite sure couldn't be inner teachers.

My experiences of these particular dream visitors are that they are very different from some aspect of our personality. As with all dream characters they are coming to reflect and teach but with these unusual presences it seems we are encountering something entirely different from anything we experience in ordinary reality... something wholly other than ourselves... something wholly Other... the numinous.

Theologian Rudolph Otto calls these an encounter with the "mysterium tremendum et fascinans," Latin for the fearful and fascinating mystery. The dream presences can evoke awe, terror, wonder and silence... and yet even in our terror we are fascinated. They most definitely get out attention!

They have this quality of evoking simultaneously fear and awe... terror and fascination. Do we feel the urge to turn away from them, even run away? Are they so outrageous that we are certain they could not be the divine?

Hanging in 'my midnight loft' is a bronze plaque with a quote that was also inscribed over Carl Jung's door, "Vocatus Atque Non Vocatus, Deus Adept"... "Bidden or Not Bidden God Is Present."

Bidden or not bidden, each night in our dreams, the archetypes show up. They come to teach us, to expose us to ourselves ... to help us heal and repair...to recover our true self ... our soul. They come to remind us how much we are loved and how much inner support we have. For me they are agents of the divine, members of that relentless posse of curious characters who want to bring us in ... who want to bring us back home.

What is wonderful ... *and terrifying* ... about them is they will do whatever it takes to get our attention. They will come as beings of light, glowing characters that fill us with love and awe. They may come as a loving father or mother figure, a gentle or intense lover, a supportive friend.

But perhaps their greatest gift is they are willing to come in ways that startle, frighten and rattle our sense of self. Their love for us is so fierce that they will come in whatever form necessary to grab us and shake us out of our complacency and complicity ... be it a drunken homeless man who approaches us on the dream street, the guy breaking into our home, the overtly sexual stranger, the wild-haired woman challenging our need to control...*the very one we are sure could not be an archetype*. Our healing means that much to them. I have come to trust that they will put on any garment it takes to bring us to consciousness, to return us to relationship, to heal us back into the love.

Next time you have a dream where you encounter a being such as this, where upon awakening you ask, "Who was that guy?" perhaps take a breath and return to that moment...to that feeling they evoked in us. In that breath we can take another look...we were very likely in the presence of the numinous.

Who of us would approach someone every night, thousands of times, for decades, only to know we will be ignored and forgotten come morning? Most of us would turn and walk away, but the archetypes don't. I can only imagine their joy when we do begin to listen to our dreams, begin to be in relationship with them and begin to learn from them what they have to teach us.

CHAPTER 10

ALIGNMENT

Coming full circle to what I said in the first chapter, our dreams want to show us how our inner self and outer self are or are not in alignment. In our willingness to work with what we're being shown about ourselves we slowly start to change. The inner and outer start to come into alignment. Then we experience the miracle of living in the outer world from our inner true self. We come into true relationship with ourselves, others and the divine from the essence of who we are... our soul self.

As we come into alignment we get to lay down all the armament of persona that we thought we needed to protect ourselves. The qualities of our soul, our vulnerability, love, capacity to feel the full range of essential feelings now find expression in the world... and we and the world are better for it.

As we come into alignment we learn to recognize the archetypes in our dreams and even welcome their outrageous reality-challenging behavior.

We learn to bring our awareness of them to our waking reality. We begin to notice archetypal moments, invitations to be in relationship with something larger than ourselves in our outer world... and be open to what they might be wanting to teach us.

We get to be aware of, delighted with, and humbled by those moments of synchronicity, of the numinous events that occur in our waking reality. The lines between inner and outer for that moment become blurred and we get to be in the archetypal world. We think of a beloved and the phone rings and it's them. Our hearts turn to the thought of a loved one who has passed and a wind chime rings on a breezeless day. We fall asleep with an inner conflict and awaken in the early dawn with an incredibly clear response.

And sometimes we are aware of this archetypal world in fellow humans... where... if we can take a breath, a pause and look through our inner eyes.

A really sweet personal example of this is something that happened to me over twenty years ago and has stayed with me:

I was standing in front of the classroom, my Spanish III class about to begin, the late bell had already rung. Just as I was about to greet the class with my perfectly paced, on task tight lesson plan... in walked a student I'll call Brent.

Brent was one of the gentlest, most unique teens I've ever known. He was what used to be referred to as an alternative student, that is someone who was on the edge of the mainstream, never quite fitting into the very college prep environment of a large suburban high school. Brent wasn't a strong student academically but he was sweet, polite and creative; everyone liked him. If caught smoking, which was almost daily, he'd just come along to the dean without an argument. I genuinely liked this kid. Whatever his personal myth was, it certainly was an interesting one.

So, into class strolls Brent, late, in his bopping walk, ubiquitous half smile ... and looped from a thick metal chain on his belt was the heavy cast iron grate from a stove top.

Thirty pairs of eyes looked at Brent ... thirty pairs of eyes turned back and looked at me to see what I would do. Late ... no pass ... supposed to write him up ... all I could do was hold back the laugh that wanted to burst out of me but didn't as I didn't want to embarrass him. In that outrageously archetypal moment I was jolted out of my perfectly timed class opening, my responsibility to follow the rules, teach bell to bell ... and I was dropped into a world that was upside down and hilarious. If Brent wasn't at that moment an archetype in the flesh, then I don't know who could be. The whole class, including me and Brent, smiled in delight at each other as if in that moment we all got some cosmic inside joke, shared a collective sigh and began class in a more otherworldly frame of mind.

> *"We fall asleep and show up for work.*
> *Drifting off, we slide out of this body and into a*
> *luminous lab coat to continue our research in the*
> *laboratory."*
> —Stephen Levine from *"Turning Towards the Mystery"*

Working with our dreams, learning from them isn't a guarantee that we will magically repair and return to our soul self…and maybe it is. My dream blog is called *Dreams: The Sacred Experiment*. Each night I get to step into the mystery that is the dream, I get to be a student of those guys, that curious cast of characters and each morning I get to open and accept their invitation to come home to my soul.

.

ACKNOWLEDGEMENTS

In my desire to publish a revised edition of *Who Are those Guys?* I knew I didn't want to go it alone, that I wanted the support and expertise of professionals.

I couldn't be more pleased with the inspiration that Andrew Shurtz brought to the pages of this work. Andrew's thoughtful suggestions made real the changes I was hoping for including the fonts for the title and chapter headings, which are the same as the original film poster for "Butch Cassidy and the Sundance Kid." I am grateful for Andrew's combined capacity for whimsy and elegance.

And my first choice to create the new cover was the incredibly talented and creative artist, Greg Miles. Our first meeting was less about the cover itself and more about dreams and the many characters who populate them each night. Our subsequent conversations were alive with how and why our dreams come to us. Greg brought those images and feelings to life in the new cover. I utterly love it.

During the process of learning to work with my own dreams and those of my clients I was fortunate to work with a number of dream teachers, all of whom I am grateful to for their insights and their teachings.

There is one, however, with whom I work my own dreams, who has been with me in this descent work from the beginning and that is my teacher, Rodger Kamenetz. Each step of the rocky way, through my moments of heels dug in resistance, angry reactions, messy projections, the whole of Pandora's box that my dreams opened up, Rodger kept a steady hand on the rudder of my dreams. He didn't get pulled off course by my reactions and rationale...he didn't get distracted by the surface story...he listened to the dream and more importantly, he listened to the archetypes. My descent to my soul and my relationship with the archetypes continues to deepen. As parts of me are repaired and I recover my ability to love and be loved, recover my soul's capacity to feel it all, it does not come without struggle and pain. Yet each step of the way I know I can look over and feel the presence of all my teachers. I have the support and encouragement of my outer teacher, Rodger, the support of my inner teachers, the archetypes...and my own precious soul.

I cannot imagine that I could be doing this work without a partner and a fan such as I have in my husband, Joe. He knew going in when we were young teens that my spiritual path was my heart's desire. Some of what my inner work entails is also his own inner work. Much of it, he will be the first to admit, he doesn't understand. Maybe that is the very reason why he is such a trusted support and partner. I rarely have to explain let alone defend what it is I need to do as Joe's love for me and trust in what it is I am called to do outweighs his own fears and hesitancies. He is excited to witness and be a part of this journey with me as I am his.

Finally, I am grateful to this curious cast of characters who come into my dreams every night and include the archetypes. However they choose to portray themselves in the service of repairing my soul connection, I know they do it with love, humor and a fierce desire to be in relationship. Working with my dreams, welcoming them, trusting them, and loving them I no longer ask 'Who are those guys?' Instead I've learned to ask, "What do you guys want to teach me? I'll do whatever it takes."

ABOUT THE AUTHOR

Mary Jo Heyen, M.Ed., is a certified practitioner of Natural Dreamwork. She works with dream clients one-on-one throughout the country and internationally, either in person, phone or Skype. She teaches a wide variety of dream-related presentations and workshops. Her work also includes being a hospice volunteer, their dream specialist, working with the dreams and visions of the dying, their families and grief groups. As a long time meditation practitioner and teacher Mary Jo also integrates meditation and dreamwork for those dreamers who practice both as each practice supports and deepens the other.

Her work with dreams has been featured in DreamTime Magazine, a publication of the International Association for the Study of Dreams (IASD) where she also serves as a Regional Representative. Her hospice work with the dreams and visions of the dying has been published in The Journal of Palliative Medicine. She was a featured dream teacher on the Shift Network's 2019 Dreamwork Summit.

Mary Jo and her husband, Joe, live in the beautiful Rocky Mountains of Colorado.

Contact Mary Jo at her dream website www.maryjoheyen.com.

Made in the USA
Monee, IL
01 February 2020